GW00646807

Mon imagier anglais

Apprends l'anglais avec Daisy, Ben et Keekee !

HarperCollins Publishers

Westerhill Road
Bishopbriggs
Glasgow
G64 2QT

Première édition/First edition 2012

Reprint 10 9 8 7 6 5 4 3 2

© HarperCollins Publishers 2012

ISBN 978-2-32100-096-9

Collins ® is a registered trademark of HarperCollins Publishers Limited

www.collinslanguage.com

A catalogue record for this book is available from the British Library

Imprimé et relié par/Printed and bound in China by South China Printing Co. Ltd

**Contenu développé et compilé par/
Content developed and compiled by
Karen Jamieson**

Dictionnaires Le Robert
25 avenue Pierre-de-Coubertin
75211 Paris cedex 13
www.lerobert.fr
Dépôt légal mars 2012

Conception graphique et artistique de/
Artwork and design by Q2AMedia

Musique et paroles de/Music and lyrics by
Iskra Anguelova

Songs arranged and produced by
www.tomdickanddebbie.com

Photocomposition supplémentaire de/
Additional typesetting by
Davidson Publishing Solutions, Glasgow

For the publisher:
Lucy Cooper   Kerry Ferguson   Elaine Higgleton
Laurent Jouet   Kate Nicholson   Lisa Sutherland

Cet ouvrage est accompagné d'un CD audio contenant des chansons et les mots prononcés. En voici le détail :

1. Say the alphabet!
2. Chanson: I can count!
3. Mots: I can count!
4. Chanson: Colour fun
5. Mots: Colour fun
6. Chanson: Shape search
7. Mots: Shape search.
8. Chanson: My body and face
9. Mots: My body and face
10. Chanson: How I feel
11. Mots: How I feel
12. Chanson: My family at home
13. Mots: My family at home
14. Chanson: Things I do
15. Mots: Things I do
16. Chanson: More things I do
17. Mots: More things I do
18. Chanson: What's it like?
19. Mots: What's it like?
20. Chanson: My day
21. Mots: My day
22. Chanson: Playtime
23. Mots: Playtime
24. Chanson: My classroom
25. Mots: My classroom
26. Chanson: Art time
27. Mots: Art time
28. Chanson: Music time
29. Mots: Music time
30. Chanson: My bedtime
31. Mots: My bedtime
32. Chanson: The fruit stall
33. Mots: The fruit stall
34. Chanson: Supermarket visit
35. Mots: Supermarket visit
36. Chanson: Breakfast time
37. Mots: Breakfast time
38. Chanson: Lunchtime
39. Mots: Lunchtime
40. Chanson: A special dinner
41. Mots: A special dinner
42. Chanson: Baking day
43. Mots: Baking day
44. Chanson: My birthday party
45. Mots: My birthday party
46. Chanson: My pets
47. Mots: My pets
48. Chanson: On the farm
49. Mots: On the farm
50. Chanson: Safari sports day
51. Mots: Safari sports day
52. Chanson: Jungle soccer
53. Mots: Jungle soccer
54. Chanson: In the sea
55. Mots: In the sea
56. Chanson: Rock pool band
57. Mots: Rock pool band
58. Chanson: Bugs and mini-beasts
59. Mots: Bugs and mini-beasts
60. Chanson: The weather
61. Mots: The weather
62. Chanson: Summer clothes
63. Mots: Summer clothes
64. Chanson: Winter clothes
65. Mots: Winter clothes
66. Chanson: My town
67. Mots: My town
68. Chanson: My house and garden
69. Mots: My house and garden
70. Chanson: In the park with grandpa
71. Mots: In the park with grandpa
72. Chanson: Fairytale castle
73. Mots: Fairytale castle

Contents

The alphabet 2
L'alphabet 2

I can count! 4
Je sais compter ! 4

Colour fun 6
Jeux de couleurs 6

Shape search 8
Retrouve les formes 8

My body and face 10
Mon corps et mon visage 10

How I feel 12
Ce que je ressens 12

My family at home 14
Ma famille à la maison 14

Things I do 16
Les choses que je fais 16

More things I do 18
D'autres choses que je fais 18

What's it like? 20
C'est comment ? 20

My day 22
Ma journée 22

Play time 24
Place au jeu ! 24

My classroom 26
Ma salle de classe 26

Art time 28
Le cours de dessin 28

Music time 30
Le cours de musique 30

My bedtime 32
L'heure du coucher 32

The fruit stall 34
Chez le marchand de fruits 34

Supermarket visit 36
Au supermarché 36

Breakfast time 38
Le petit-déjeuner 38

Lunchtime 40
Le déjeuner 40

A special dinner 42
Un dîner spécial 42

Baking day 44
On fait des gâteaux 44

My birthday party 46
Ma fête d'anniversaire 46

My pets 48
Mes animaux de compagnie 48

On the farm 50
À la ferme 50

Safari sports day 52
Les jeux de la savane 52

Jungle soccer 54
Le foot de la jungle 54

In the sea 56
Dans la mer 56

Rock pool band 58
L'orchestre sous-marin 58

Bugs and mini-beasts 60
Insectes et petites bêtes 60

The weather 62
Le temps qu'il fait 62

Summer clothes 64
Vêtements d'été 64

Winter clothes 66
Vêtements d'hiver 66

My town 68
Ma ville 68

My house and garden 70
Ma maison et son jardin 70

In the park with grandpa 72
Au parc avec Papy 72

Fairytale castle 74
Un château de conte de fée 74

Index 76

The alphabet

Aa Bb Cc

Dd Ee Ff

Gg Hh Ii

Jj Kk Ll

2

Mm Nn Oo

Pp Qq Rr

Ss Tt Uu

Vv Ww Xx

Yy Zz

I can count!

1 one
un

2 two
deux

3 three
trois

4 four
quatre

5 five
cinq

Activities

1. Can you count to 10?
2. Sing the song!

Song

1, 2, 3, 4, 5
1, 2, 3, 4, 5

6 six
six

7 seven
sept

8 eight
huit

9 nine
neuf

10 ten
dix

I can count, I can count,
I can count to five!

6, 7, 8, 9, 10
6, 7, 8, 9, 10

Can you count? Can you count,
Can you count to ten? YES!

5

Colour fun

white — blanc

blue bleu

green vert

Activities

1. Find the hidden snake.
2. Sing the song!

Song

Yellow and blue (x4)
make the green of the trees. (x2)

black
noir

purple
violet

red
rouge

yellow
jaune

orange
orange

Yellow and red (x4)
make the orange of the sun. (x2)

Red and blue (x4)
make the purple of the grapes. (x2)

Shape search

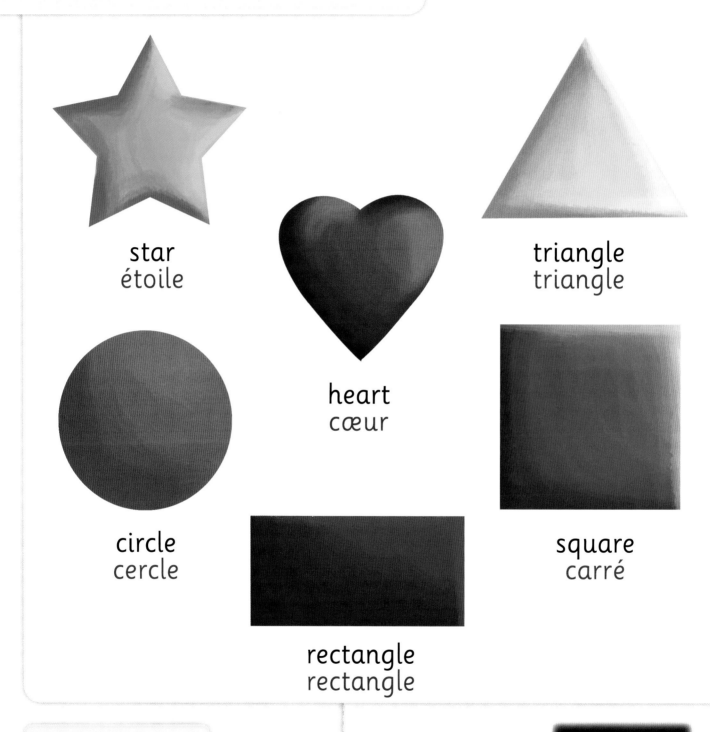

star
étoile

heart
cœur

triangle
triangle

circle
cercle

square
carré

rectangle
rectangle

Activities

1. Find the hidden mouse.
2. Sing the song!

Song

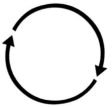 

Round and round the circle goes.
The star shines in the sky.

Count the shapes

Three sides make a triangle.
A heart says 'I love you'.

The square is
like a window.

The rectangle's
like a door. (x2)

My body and face

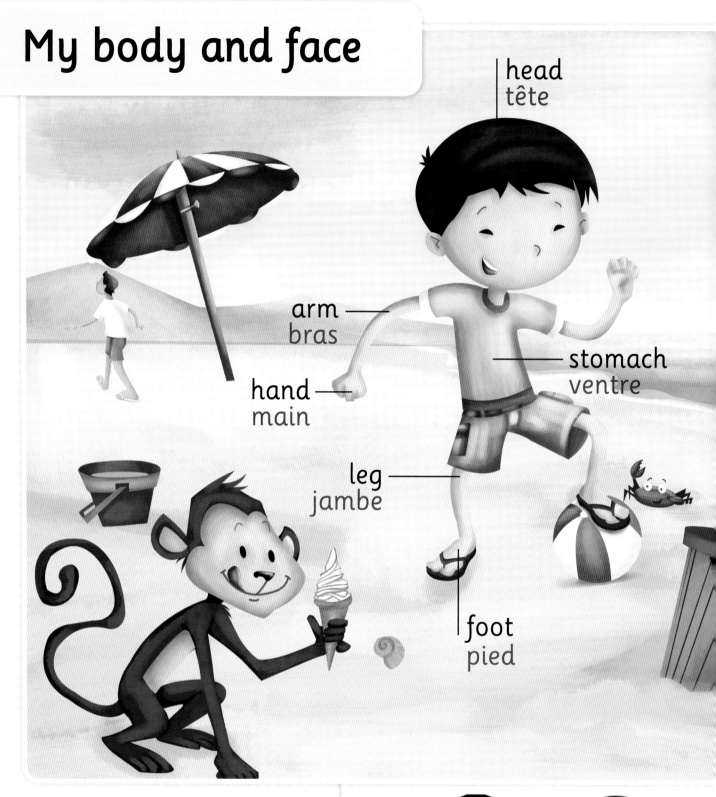

head
tête

arm
bras

hand
main

stomach
ventre

leg
jambe

foot
pied

Activities

1. Find the hidden elephant.
2. Sing the song!

Song

One nose,

One mouth,

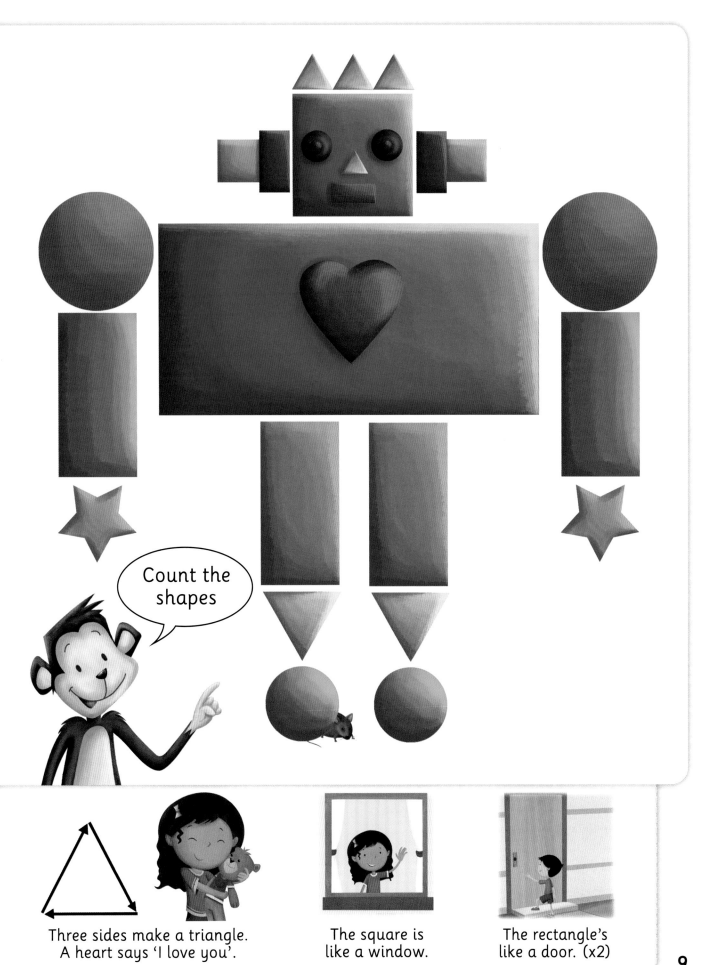

Count the shapes

Three sides make a triangle.
A heart says 'I love you'.

The square is
like a window.

The rectangle's
like a door. (x2)

9

My body and face

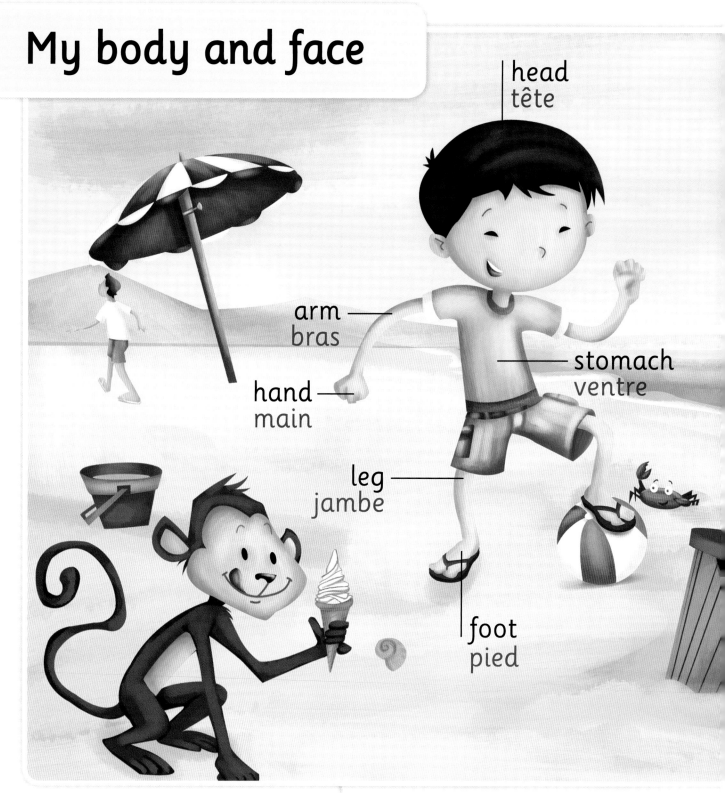

head
tête

arm
bras

hand
main

stomach
ventre

leg
jambe

foot
pied

Activities

1. Find the hidden elephant.
2. Sing the song!

Song

One nose,

One mouth,

hair
cheveux

nose
nez

eye
œil

ear
oreille

mouth
bouche

Two eyes,

Two ears. (x 2)

Hair, hair, hair,
hair everywhere!

Hair, hair, hair,
hair everywhere!

How I feel

angry
en colère

sad
triste

happy
heureuse

tired
fatiguée

Activities

1. Find the hidden apple.
2. Sing the song!

Song

I am hungry. (x 2)
Hamburgers, fries!

12

hungry
affamé

thirsty
assoiffé

scared
effrayé

shy
timide

I am thirsty. (x 2)
Pour me some milk!

I am happy. (x 2)
Cuddle my cat!

I am tired. (x 2)
Let's go to bed!

My family at home

grandma
mamie

grandpa
papy

Activities

1. Find the hidden parrot.
2. Who lives with you?
3. Sing the song!

Song

Look at mummy! Look at daddy!

daddy
papa

brother
frère

mummy
maman

me!
moi !

sister
sœur

There's my sister,
baby brother.

Look at grandma! Look
at grandpa! Look at me!

This is my family!

Things I do

stand up
se lever

sit down
s'asseoir

touch my toes
toucher ses orteils

jump
sauter

Activities

1. Find the hidden teddy.
2. Sing the song!

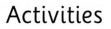

Song

Sit down, Daisy,
drink some juice. (x 2)
Sit down Daisy.

16

eat
manger

drink
boire

cry
pleurer

laugh
rire

Stand up Ben, and
eat some grapes. (x 2)
Stand up, Ben.

Jump up, high,
then touch your toes. (x 2)
Jump up, Keekee.

Don't cry, Daisy!
Laugh with Ben. (x 2)
Don't cry, Daisy!

More things I do

hold hands
donner la main

wave
saluer

run
courir

walk
marcher

Activities

1. Find the hidden shell.
2. Sing the song!

Song

Let's make a circle! (x 2)
All hold hands! (x 2)

18

clap
applaudir

turn around
se retourner

rub my tummy
se frotter le ventre

make a circle
se mettre en rond

Turn around! (x 2)
Clap your hands! (x 2)

Here is your mummy! (x 2)
Run, run, run! (x 2)

Here is your mummy! (x 2)
Run, run, run! (x 2) Run!

What's it like?

slow
lent

fast
rapide

small
petit

big
grand

Activities

1. Find the hidden train.
2. Sing the song!

Song

The rabbit is fast and
the turtle is slow.

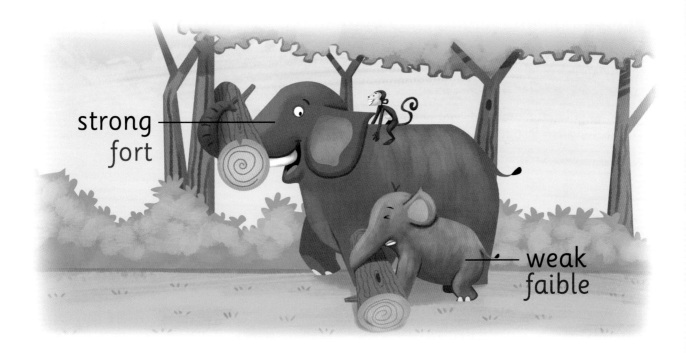

strong
fort

weak
faible

dirty
sale

clean
propre

The elephant's strong and the baby's weak.

The monkey's small, the gorilla's big!

Dirty hippo! Dirty hippo! Wash it clean!

My day

time to get up
le lever

time to get dressed
le moment de s'habiller

time for school
*l'heure d'aller
à l'école*

playtime
la récréation

snack time
le déjeuner

Activities

1. Find the hidden kangaroo.
2. Sing the song!

Song

Good morning! Good morning!
It's time to get up! (x 2)

story time
le moment d'écouter une histoire

home time
l'heure de rentrer

bath time
l'heure du bain

bedtime
le coucher

The school bell is ringing!
It's time for school! (x 2)

The water is lovely!
It's bath time, it's bath time! (x 2)

Good night! Good night!
It's bedtime! It's bedtime! (x 2)

Playtime

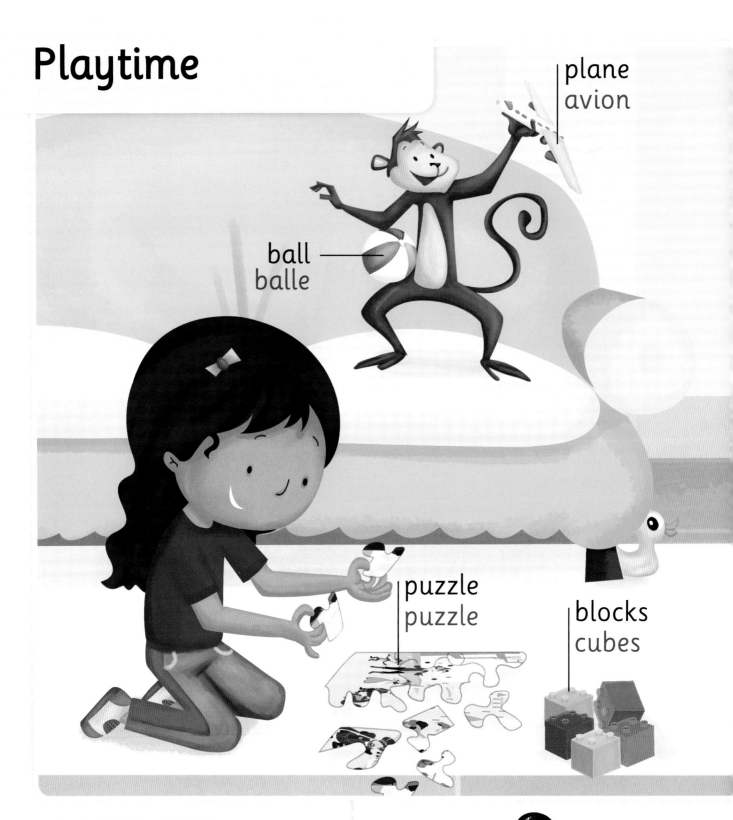

plane
avion

ball
balle

puzzle
puzzle

blocks
cubes

Activities

1. Find the hidden duck.
2. What is your favourite toy?
3. Sing the song!

Song

What's in the toy box?
(x 2)

toy box
coffre à jouets

doll
poupée

panda bear
panda

train
train

fire engine
camion de pompiers

rocket
fusée

Doll, panda bear,
train.

Rocket and ball,
puzzle and plane,

doll, panda bear,
train. (x 2)

25

My classroom

teacher
maîtresse

computer
ordinateur

a b c

whiteboard
tableau blanc

exercise book
cahier d'exercices

girl
fille

chair
chaise

Activities

1. Find the hidden birthday cake.
2. Sing the song!

Song

Girls and boys, girls and boys,

toys
jouets

boy
garçon

table
table

books
livres

bag
sac

sit on your chairs!

Open your books! (x 2)

a b c

Look at the teacher,
at the whiteboard! (x 4)

Art time

paper
papier

crayons
crayons
de couleur

glue
colle

scissors
ciseaux

Activities

1. Find the hidden rabbit.
2. Sing the song!

Song

Paper and crayons, markers and brush.
We're painting pictures. This is art class!

marker
marqueur

pencils
crayons

brush
pinceau

paint
peinture

Keekee is drawing. Ben's painting, too.
Daisy is pasting a star with some glue.

Paper and crayons, markers and brush.
We're painting pictures. This is art time!

Music time

keyboard
clavier

triangle
triangle

trumpet
trompette

drum
tambour

Activities

1. Find the hidden pair of scissors.
2. Sing the song!

Song

Let's play music! (x 2)
The violin and xylophone,
the triangle and drum! (x 2)

violin
violon

xylophone
xylophone

guitar
guitare

tambourine
tambourin

Drum, drum, Keekee,
play the drum!

Daisy plays the
trumpet! Ben - the
tambourine! (x 2)

Drum, drum, Keekee,
play the drum!

My bedtime

1. have a shower
me doucher

3. put on my pyjamas
mettre mon pyjama

2. dry myself
me sécher

4. brush my teeth
me brosser les dents

5. brush my hair
me brosser les cheveux

Activities

1. Find the hidden cat.
2. Sing the song!

Song

At the end of the day,
I put on my pyjamas,
brush my teeth, brush my hair.

6. go to the toilet
aller aux toilettes

7. wash my hands
me laver les mains

8. get into bed
me mettre au lit

9. cuddle my teddy
faire un câlin à mon nounours

10. kiss goodnight
dire bonne nuit

At the end of the day,
I get into bed, cuddle my teddy
and kiss him goodnight.

Kiss my mummy,
say goodnight.
(x 2)

At the end of the day,
I get into bed, cuddle my teddy
and say goodnight!

The fruit stall

watermelons
pastèques

pears
poires

strawberries
fraises

pineapples
ananas

oranges
oranges

Activities

1. Find the hidden seahorse.
2. What is your favourite fruit?
3. Sing the song!

Song

I like peaches,
I like pears.

34

grapes
raisin

cherries
cerises

peaches
pêches

apples
pommes

bananas
bananes

Keekee likes
bananas. (x 2)

Watermelon,
apples, grapes,

oranges and cherries!
(x 2)

Supermarket visit

lettuces
laitues

mushrooms
champignons

carrots
carottes

cucumbers
concombres

red peppers
poivrons rouges

Activities

1. Find the hidden train.
2. Which vegetables do you like best?
3. Sing the song!

Song

Daddy's got a basket. (x 2)

potatoes
pommes
de terre

broccoli
brocolis

green peppers
poivrons verts

onions
oignons

tomatoes
tomates

basket
panier

Carrots, lettuce, mushrooms,
onions, broccoli.

Daddy's got a
basket. (x 2)

Carrots, lettuce, mushrooms,
onions, broccoli.

37

Breakfast time

toast
pain
grillé

tea
thé

yoghurt
yaourt

cup
tasse

Activities

1. Find the hidden paintbrush.
2. What do you have for breakfast?
3. Sing the song!

Song

Milk and cereal, bread and jam,
Daisy likes to eat. (x 2)

coffee
café

cereal
céréales

milk
lait

juice
jus

spoon
cuillère

honey
miel

bread
pain

jam
confiture

Mummy, mummy, pass me the honey!
Daddy, daddy, give me the toast!

Milk and cereal, bread and jam,
Daisy likes to eat.

Lunchtime

sushi
sushi

chocolate
chocolat

chicken
poulet

egg rolls
pâtés
impériaux

tacos
tacos

noodles
nouilles

At school

Activities

1. Find the hidden flower.
2. What's your favourite food?
3. Sing the song!

Song

I am hungry! I am hungry
– some pizza, please!

cheese
fromage

salad
salade

meat sauce
sauce bolognaise

pizza
pizza

corn
maïs

pasta
pâtes

At home

Mummy, pass me, mummy, pass me, salad and corn!

Noodles, tacos, chicken, sushi, chocolate and cheese!

I am hungry, I am hungry! It's time for lunch.

A special dinner

steak
steak

peas
petits pois

rice
riz

fork
fourchette

knife
couteau

fish
poisson

ketchup
ketchup

Activities

1. Find the hidden flower.
2. Sing the song!

Song

Rice and fish,
steak and peas,

fries
frites

hamburger
hamburger

soup
soupe

baked potato
pomme de
terre au four

beans
haricots

I'm so hungry, give me
some, please! (x 2)

Hamburger, fries, baked
potatoes, beans

I'm so hungry, give me
some, please! (x 2)

43

Baking day

butter
beurre

syrup
sirop

flour
farine

plate
assiette

Activities

1. Find the hidden sunglasses.
2. Sing the song!

Song

Mummy's baking cookies.

cookies
cookies

oven
four

bowl
bol

sugar
sucre

eggs
œufs

Daisy's cracking eggs.

Butter, flour, syrup.

This is baking day.

My birthday party

birthday present
cadeau d'anniversaire

ice cream
glace

birthday
card
carte
d'anniversaire

Activities

1. Find the hidden bee.
2. Can you count the candles on the cake?
3. Sing the song!

Song

Are you ready for the party? (x 2)

Presents, cards, balloons! (x 3)

balloons
ballons

popcorn
pop-corn

sandwiches
sandwiches

cake
gâteau

water
eau

sweets
bonbons

fruit
fruits

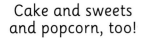

Cake and sweets
and popcorn, too!

Ice cream, water,
fruit! (x 2)

Are you ready for
the party? (x 2)

Presents, cards,
balloons! (x 3)

My pets

dog
chien

puppy
chiot

hamster
hamster

guinea-pig
cochon d'Inde

Activities

1. Find the hidden umbrella.
2. Can you hop like a rabbit and stretch like a cat?
3. Sing the song!

Song

Ben and Daisy have some pets:
cat, dog, rabbit. (x 2)

48

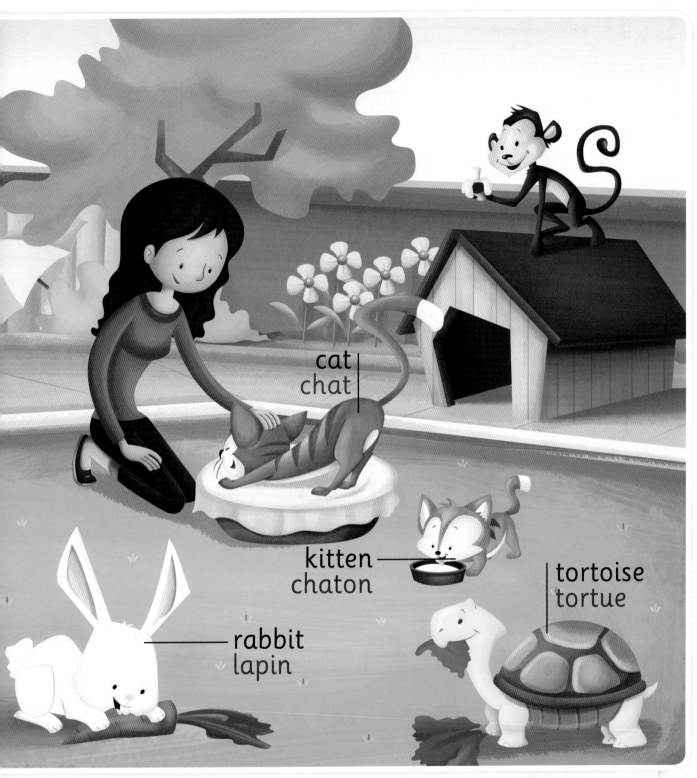

cat
chat

kitten
chaton

rabbit
lapin

tortoise
tortue

Puppy, hamster, guinea pig! (x 2)

Ben and Daisy have some pets:
cat, dog, rabbit!

On the farm

chicken
poule

donkey
âne

goose
oie

duck
canard

Activities

1. Find the hidden octopus.
2. Can you make farm animal noises?
3. Sing the song!

Song

The goose and the duck (x 2) live on the farm, on the farm.

cow
vache

horse
cheval

rat
rat

mouse
souris

sheep
mouton

The cow and the horse (x 2)
live on the farm as well.

Donkey, chicken,
sheep and mouse
play along with them.

The cow and the horse (x 2)
live on the farm, on the farm.

Safari sports day

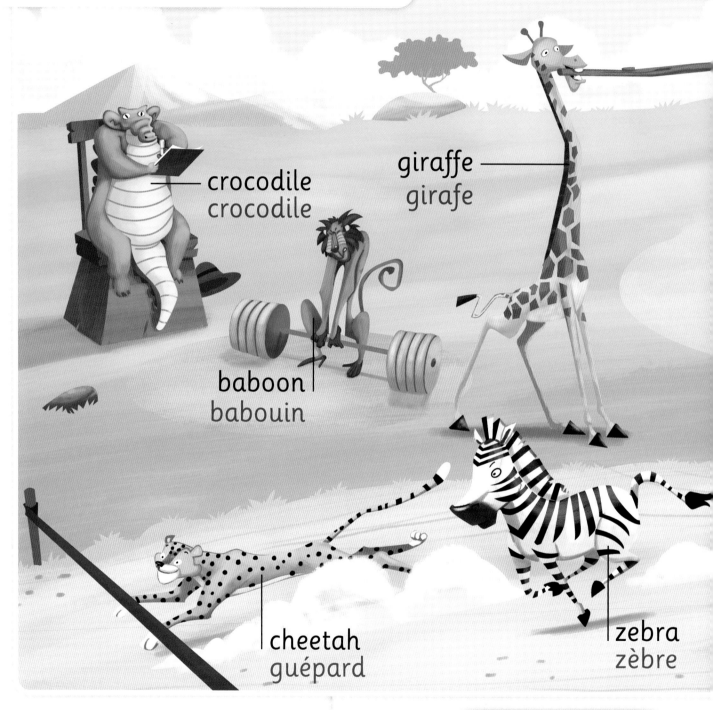

crocodile
crocodile

giraffe
girafe

baboon
babouin

cheetah
guépard

zebra
zèbre

Activities

1. Find the hidden hat.
2. Sing the song!

Song

The cheetah and the zebra,
the hippo and the rhino.

lion
lion

elephant
éléphant

hippo
hippopotame

rhino
rhinocéros

Run, run, running down the road! (x 2)

The lion's jumping over the stick! Jump! Jump! Jump! Jump! (x 2)

Jungle soccer

snake
serpent

gorilla
gorille

tiger
tigre

monkey
singe

chimpanzee
chimpanzé

Activities

1. Find the hidden drum.
2. Sing the song!

Song

Jungle soccer is
the game

parrot
perroquet

orang-utan
orang-outang

leopard
léopard

iguana
iguane

gorillas and orang-utans
like to play! (x 2)

Monkeys, tigers
and chimpanzees,

kick the ball and play
with me! (x 2)

In the sea

dolphin
dauphin

shark
requin

seal
phoque

octopus
pieuvre

shipwreck
épave

Activities

1. Find the hidden school bag.
2. Sing the song!

Song

In the sea, in the sea
lives a dolphin.

walrus
morse

whale
baleine

penguin
pingouin

turtle
tortue

In the sea, in the sea
live his friends.

The octopus, the penguin,
the seal and the turtle,

all live in the sea! (x 2)

57

Rock pool band

jellyfish
méduse

starfish
étoile de mer

shell
coquillage

rock
rocher

Activities

1. Find the hidden spoon.
2. Sing the song!

Song

Jellyfish, jellyfish,
play the drums!

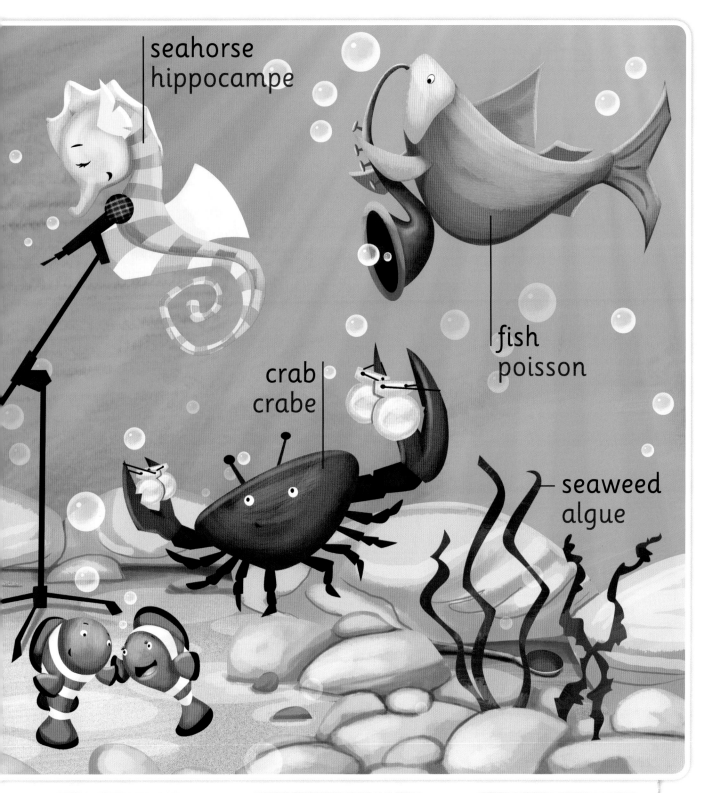

seahorse
hippocampe

fish
poisson

crab
crabe

seaweed
algue

Starfish, seahorse
sing a song!

Jellyfish, jellyfish,
play the drums!

Seaweed, crab,
join the rock pool band!

59

Bugs and mini-beasts

butterfly
papillon

bee
abeille

beetle
scarabée

ladybird
coccinelle

Activities

1. Find the hidden bananas.
2. Sing the song!

Song

Fly, fly, butterfly,

spider
araignée

caterpillar
chenille

ant
fourmi

cricket
grillon

come and see your friends! (x 2)

The little bee, the ladybird,
the caterpillar, ant! (x 2)

The weather

rainy
pluvieux

snowy
neigeux

sunny
ensoleillé

windy
venteux

Activities

1. Find the hidden tiger.
2. Colour a weather picture.
3. Sing the song!

Song

Open the umbrella!
It's rainy, it's rainy!
Open the umbrella!
It's rainy today!

cloudy
nuageux

hot
chaud

cold
froid

stormy
orageux

How the snow is falling!
It's snowy, it's snowy!
How the snow is falling!
It's snowy today!

Look the kite is flying!
It's windy, it's windy!
Look the kite is flying!
It's windy today!

How the sun is shining!
It's sunny, it's sunny!
How the sun is shining!
It's sunny today!

Summer clothes

skirt
jupe

T-shirt
t-shirt

swimming
trunks
caleçon
de bain

swimsuit
maillot
de bain

Activities

1. Find the hidden trumpet.
2. Sing the song!

Song

Sunglasses, sun hat, sandals and skirt! (x 2)

64

shirt
chemise

sunglasses
lunettes
de soleil

sun hat
chapeau

shorts
short

dress
robe

sandals
sandales

Swimming trunks and swimsuit,
T-shirt and shorts (x 2)

Summer time! Summer time!
Summer time is here! (x 2)

Winter clothes

jacket
blouson

trousers
pantalon

boots
bottes

coat
manteau

Activities

1. Find the hidden bicycle.
2. Sing the song!

Song

Mummy's wearing boots.

gloves
gants

hat
bonnet

scarf
écharpe

sweatshirt
sweat

shoes
chaussures

jeans
jean

Daisy's wearing gloves.

Ben is wearing jeans,
shoes and a hat.

Winter time is here!
(x 3)

My town

swimming pool
piscine

hairdresser
salon de coiffure

library
bibliothèque

school
école

bus
bus

motorbike
moto

bike
vélo

Activities

1. Find the hidden chimpanzee.
2. Which of these things have you seen in your town?
3. Sing the song!

Song

The swimming pool and
hairdresser,

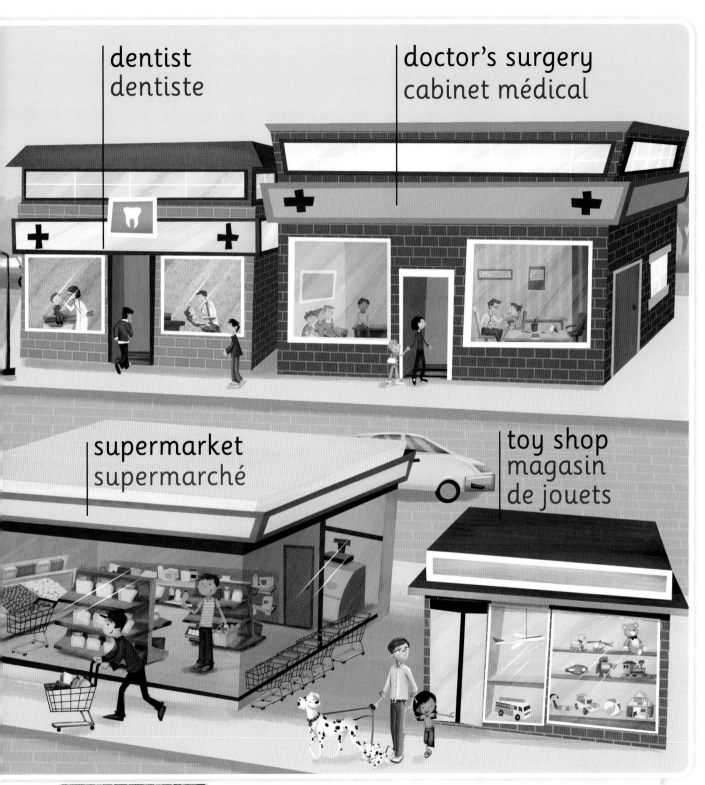

dentist
dentiste

doctor's surgery
cabinet médical

supermarket
supermarché

toy shop
magasin
de jouets

library and school.
(x 2)

Take the bus!
Ride a bike! (x 2)

To the swimming pool and
hairdresser, library and school.

69

My house and garden

tree
arbre

window
fenêtre

flower
fleur

garden
jardin

Activities

1. Find the hidden guitar.
2. Sing the song!

Song

Open the window!
Close the door! (x 2)

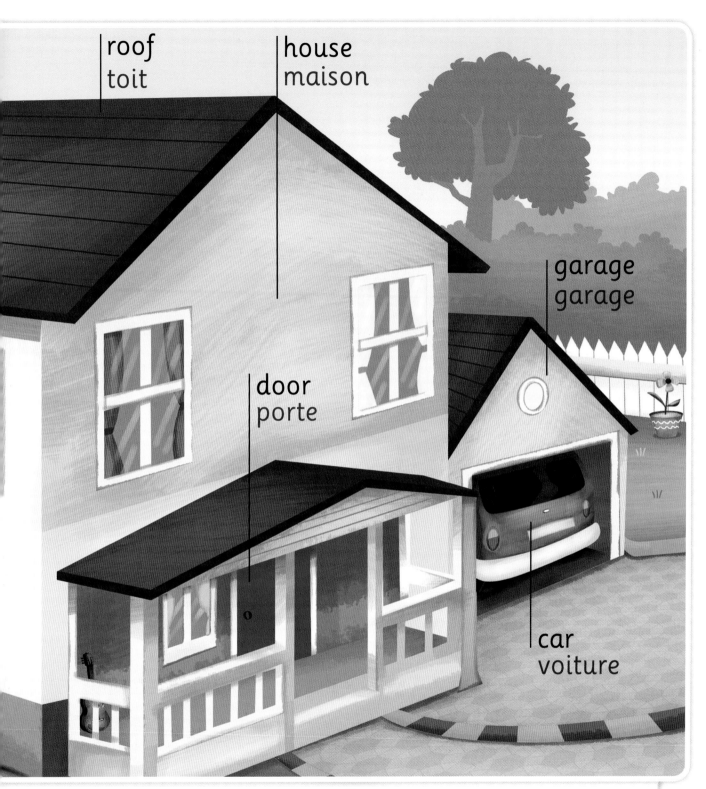

roof
toit

house
maison

garage
garage

door
porte

car
voiture

Play in the garden
with the ball! (x 2)

Flowers and trees
around the house. (x 2)

Ben and Daisy run and
play. (x 2)

In the park with grandpa

boat
bateau

lake
lac

kite
cerf-volant

kick scooter
trottinette

seesaw
bascule

Activities

1. Find the hidden tortoise.
2. Sing the song!

Song

Swing, swing,
seesaw, slide!

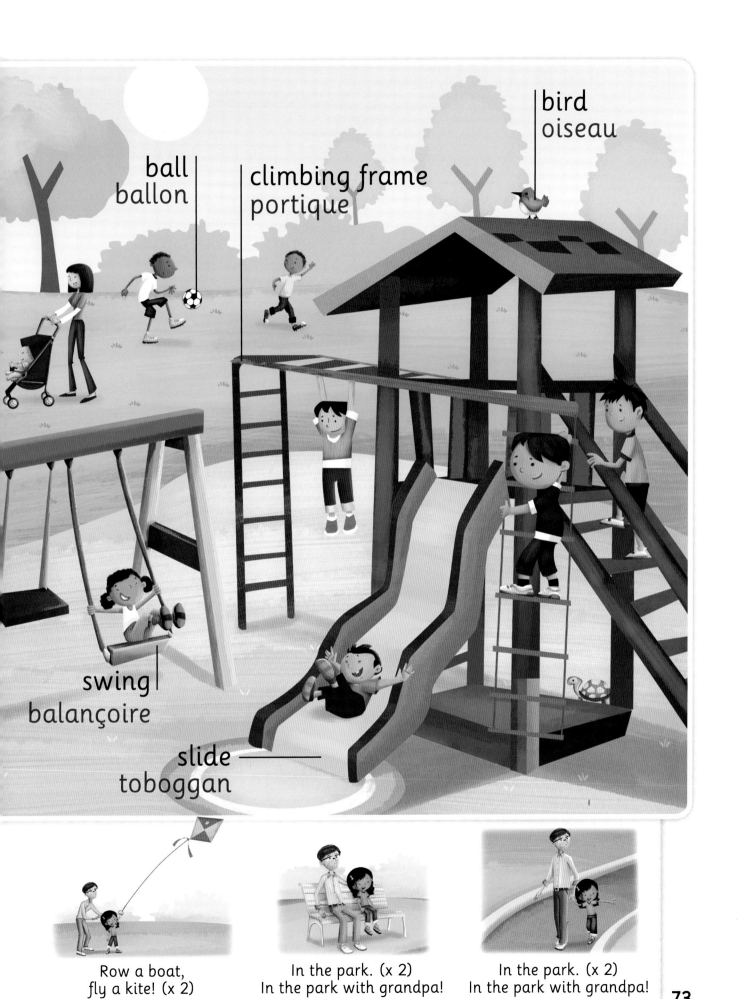

bird
oiseau

ball
ballon

climbing frame
portique

swing
balançoire

slide
toboggan

Row a boat,
fly a kite! (x 2)

In the park. (x 2)
In the park with grandpa!

In the park. (x 2)
In the park with grandpa!

Fairytale castle

prince
prince

jester
bouffon

princess
princesse

dragon
dragon

Activities

1. Find the hidden crab.
2. Sing the song!

Song

In this castle, oh, so big,

74

castle
château

knight
chevalier

minstrel
ménestrel

king
roi

queen
reine

live a princess and
a prince!

Happy minstrels play
a song,

for the king and
the queen!

75

Index

angry	12
ant	61
apple	12, 35
arm	10
baboon	52
bag	27
baked potato	43
ball	24, 73
balloons	47
bananas	35, 60
basket	37
bath time	23
beans	43
bed	33
bedtime	23, 33
bee	46, 60
beetle	60
bicycle	66
big	20
bike	68
bird	73
birthday cake	26
birthday card	46
birthday present	46
black	7
blocks	24
blue	6
boat	72
books	27
boots	66
bowl	45
boy	27
bread	39
broccoli	37
brother	15
brush	29
brush my teeth	32
bus	68
butter	44
butterfly	60
cake	47
car	71
carrots	36
castle	75
cat	32, 49
caterpillar	61
cereal	39
chair	26
cheese	41
cheetah	52
cherries	35
chicken	40, 50
chimpanzee	54, 68
chocolate	40
circle	8
clap	19
clean	21
climbing frame	73
cloudy	63
coat	66
coffee	39
cold	63
computer	26
cookies	45
corn	41
cow	51
crab	59, 74
crayons	28
cricket	61
crocodile	52
cry	17
cucumbers	36
cuddle my teddy	33
cup	38
daddy	15
dentist	69
dirty	21
doctor's surgery	69
dog	48
doll	25
dolphin	56
donkey	50
door	71
dragon	74
dress	65
drink	17
drum	30, 54
dry myself	32
duck	24, 50
ear	11
eat	17
egg rolls	40
eggs	45
eight	5
elephant	10, 33
exercise book	26
eye	11
fast	20
fire engine	25
fish	42, 59
five	4
flour	44
flower	40, 42, 70
foot	10
fork	42
four	4